HOUGHTON MIFFLIN Reading
A Legacy of Literacy

Let's Be Friends

Senior Authors
J. David Cooper
John J. Pikulski

Authors
Patricia A. Ackerman
Kathryn H. Au
David J. Chard
Gilbert G. Garcia
Claude N. Goldenberg
Marjorie Y. Lipson
Susan E. Page
Shane Templeton
Sheila W. Valencia
MaryEllen Vogt

Consultants
Linda H. Butler
Linnea C. Ehri
Carla B. Ford

 HOUGHTON MIFFLIN   BOSTON • MORRIS PLAINS, NJ

California • Colorado • Georgia • Illinois • New Jersey • Texas

Cover and page photography by Michelle Joyce

Cover illustration by Anna Rich.

Acknowledgments begin on page 156.

Printed in the U.S.A.

ISBN: 0-618-01227-3

123456789-DW-06 05 04 03 02 01 00

Contents
Theme 3

Let's Look Around! 12

nonfiction

Big Book: Counting on the Woods
by George Ella Lyon
photographs by Ann W. Olson
CCBC "Choices" Bank Street College
Best Children's Books of the Year

nonfiction

Phonics Library:
Cabs, Cabs, Cabs
Fall Naps
Pam Can Pack

Big Book: Pearl's First Prize Plant
by A. Delaney

fiction

fantasy

Phonics Library:
Lots of Picking
Bill Bird
Tim's Cat

Big Book: Hilda Hen's Scary Night
by Mary Wormell

Bank Street College Best Children's
Books of the Year

fantasy

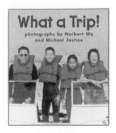

nonfiction

Phonics Library:
Let's Trim the Track
Brad's Quick Rag Tricks
Fran Pig's Brick Hut

Let's Trim
the Track!
by Rafael Lopez
illustrated by Stacey Schuett

Let's trim the grass
at the track.

On My Way Practice Reader

Mack
by James M. Pare

Apple Picking
by Irma Singer

The Crab
by Alice E. Lisson

Theme Paperbacks

Barnyard Tracks
by Dee Dee Duffy
illustrated by Janet Marshall

Mud!
by Charnan Simon
photographs by
Dorothy Handelman

When Tiny Was Tiny
by Cari Meister
illustrated by Rich Davis

Family and Friends 84

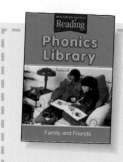

Big Book: Caribbean Dream
by Rachel Isadora

🎗 Americas Award Commended List

realistic
fiction

realistic
fiction

Phonics Library:
Buzzing Bug
Duff in the Mud
Jess and Mom

Additional Resources

On My Way Practice Reader

Family Day
by Naomi Parker

Best Friends
by Ann Takman

The Bug Jug Band
by Dan McDaniel

Theme Paperbacks

Biscuit Finds a Friend
by Alyssa Satin Capucilli
illustrated by Pat Schories

Come! Sit! Speak!
by Charnan Simon
illustrated by Bari Weissman

The Day the Sheep Showed Up
by David McPhail

To read about more good books, go to Education Place.

www.eduplace.com/kids

· ·

This Internet reading incentive program provides thousands of titles for children to read.

www.bookadventure.org

Let's Look Around!

Sleeping Outdoors

Under the dark
is a star,

Under the star
is a tree,

Under the tree
is a blanket,

And under the
blanket is me.

by Marchette Chute

Seasons

Seasons

written by Michael Medearis

Words to Know

animal	see
bird	fat
cold	nap
fall	cap
flower	sacks
full	pack
look	bugs
of	

It is fall.

Jack can get a cap.

It can get cold.

Jack can get a flower.

Jack can see a bird. Tap, tap, tap!

It can get big, fat bugs.

Look! The fat animal can nap.

Dad and Jack pack sacks full

of nuts.

Meet the Author
Michael Medearis

Seasons

written by Michael Medearis

Fall

It can get cool.

I pack ten big tan sacks full of leaves.

Birds go south.
Animals get fat, fat, fat.

20

Winter

It can get cold.

An animal can get set to nap.
It can dig a den.

Snow can fall.

Pat, pat, pat!
Look at my big snowman!

I add a tan cap and bits of coal.

Spring

It can get wet.

Tap, tap, tap!

See the sap? A bird can get bugs.

I find a flower.

Summer

It can get hot.

I sit and get wet.

Fan, fan, fan!
I am not hot.

I pack my box and get a big net.

Dad and I get a big bass.

Think About the Story

1 How do animals get ready for the different seasons?

2 What different things do people do in different seasons? Why?

3 What happens during the seasons where you live?

Write a Sentence

Write a sentence about your favorite season.

Shiny colored tents
pop up above people's heads
at the first raindrop

by **Myra Cohn Livingston**

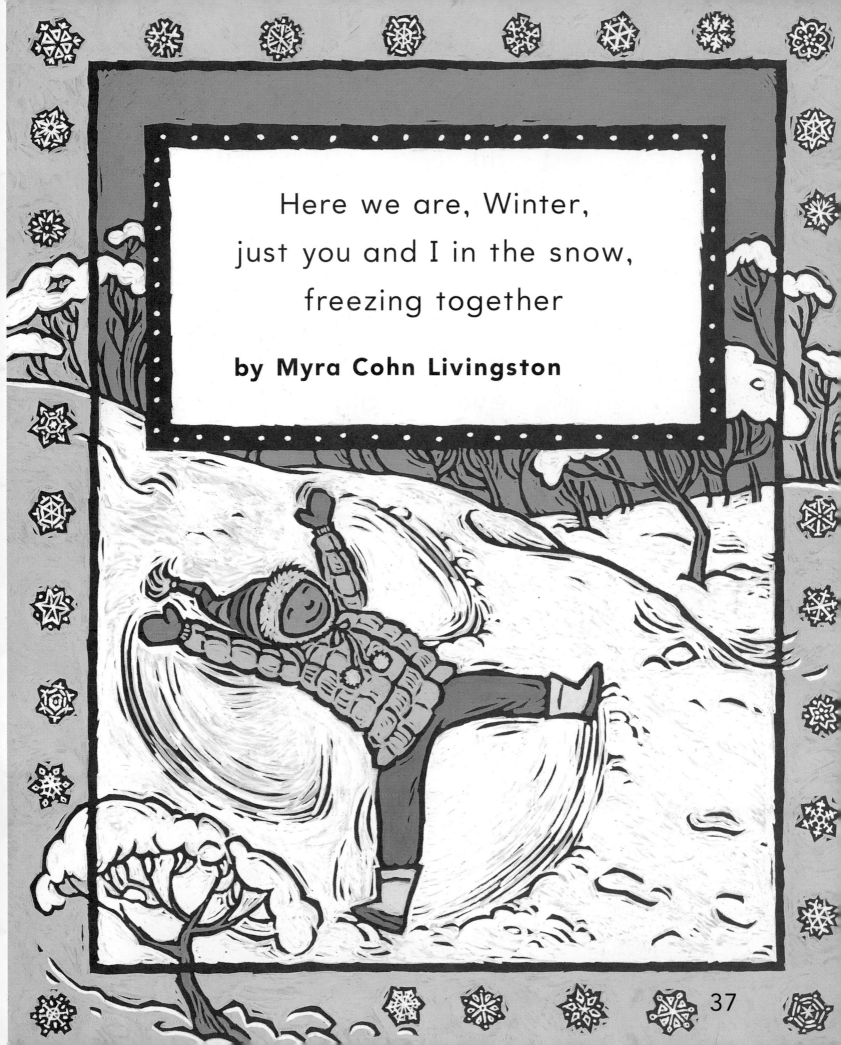

Here we are, Winter,
just you and I in the snow,
freezing together

by Myra Cohn Livingston

Mr. C's Dinner

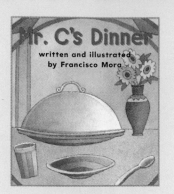

Words to Know

all	first	bib
call	never	in
why	will	lips
paper	miss	digs
eat	Pig	licked
every	big	packed
shall	six	backing

The ad in the paper said,
"Eat all you can at Big C's."

"I will call Pig," said Fox.

"Pig, why not eat at Big C's?" said Fox.

"I never miss big, big eats," said Pig.

"Shall we get to Big C's at six, Fox?"

Pig packed every bib he had.

"Who digs in first, Fox?" said Pig.

Pig licked his big lips.

"Not I, Pig," said Fox, backing away.

Meet the Author and Illustrator
Francisco Mora

Mr. C's Dinner

written and illustrated
by Francisco Mora

Hen got a paper.

Fox got a paper.

Pig got a paper.

We shall not miss it at six.

But who is Mr. C?

They all met at Mr. C's den.
A big sign said, "Mr. C's Den."

Every animal got a big bib.

Fox licked his lips.
Pig picked a big dish.

"Fox, call Mr. C," said Hen.
Fox called.

Tap, tap, tap. Mr. C looked in.

Tap, tap, tap.

"Mr. C is Coyote!" said Hen, Fox, and Pig.

"Will you eat me?" said Pig, backing away.

"Never!" said Mr. C. "It is not a big,
bad trick. Who digs in first?"

"Yams, yams, yams! Why not dig in?"
said Hen.

Think About the Story

1 Why did Mr. C send the invitation?

2 How did the animals feel when they found out who Mr. C was? Why?

3 What would you do if you got an invitation from Mr. C?

Make a List

Write a list of other foods Mr. C might serve at dinner. Make a dinner menu using your list.

How did the egg cross the road?

She scrambled across.

What are two things you can never eat for breakfast?

Lunch and supper

What do you call two banana peels?

A pair of slippers!

**Where did the hamburgers
go to dance?**

The meatball

What a Trip!

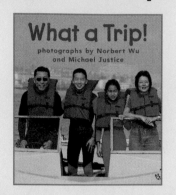

What a Trip!
photographs by Norbert Wu
and Michael Justice

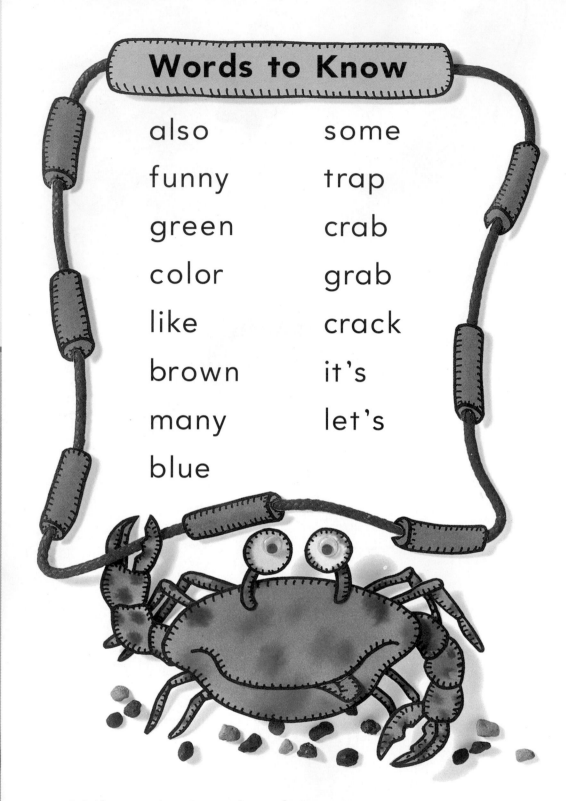

Words to Know

also	some
funny	trap
green	crab
color	grab
like	crack
brown	it's
many	let's
blue	

What is in the big wet net?

It's got some big crabs in it.

Many crabs are a blue color.

Lots of crabs are also brown.

Quick! Grab the funny brown crab!

Quick! Quick! Trap the big green crab.

Quick! Let's eat! Get set.

Crack, crack, crack! I like crabs.

Meet the Photographer
Norbert Wu

What a Trip!

**photographs by Norbert Wu
and Michael Justice**

Quick! Let's go on a trip!

Get set. Jump in.
Get wet, wet, wet!

Here is a funny big fish!
Look at its big fin! Its lips are also big!

Here is a big, fat blue fish!
It's in the sea grass.

It's a big brown crab!
Get a trap!

What can it grab?

What can it crack?

Crack, crack, crack!

What is the big green fish doing?
It's eating.

Many whales like krill.

krill

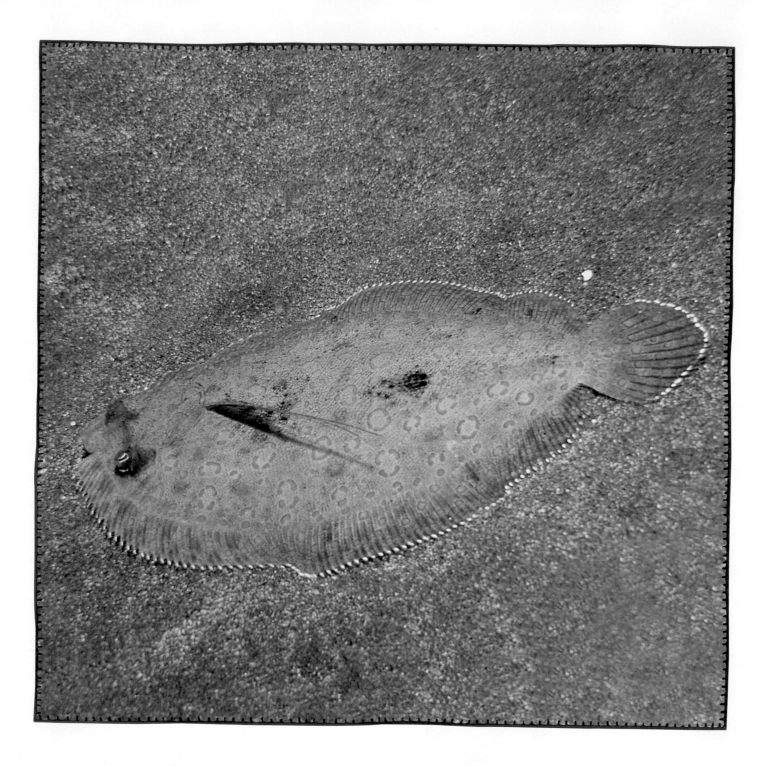

Some fish can change color.
What a trick!

Some fish can prick.
Do not grab it!

Some fish can zig zag.
Zig zag, zig zag!

Quick! Let's zig zag back.

Drip, drip, drip.
What a trip!

79

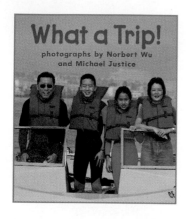

What a Trip!
photographs by Norbert Wu
and Michael Justice

Think About the Story

1 How are the fish in the story different?

2 Which fish would you like to learn more about? Why?

3 Would you like to go on a trip like this? Why?

Write a Sentence

Write a sentence about your favorite part of the story.

I liked the whale eating krill.

One, two, three, four, five

One, two, three, four, five,
Once I caught a fish alive.
Six, seven, eight, nine, ten,
Then I let it go again.

Why did you let it go?
Because it bit my finger so.
Which finger did it bite?
This little finger on my right.

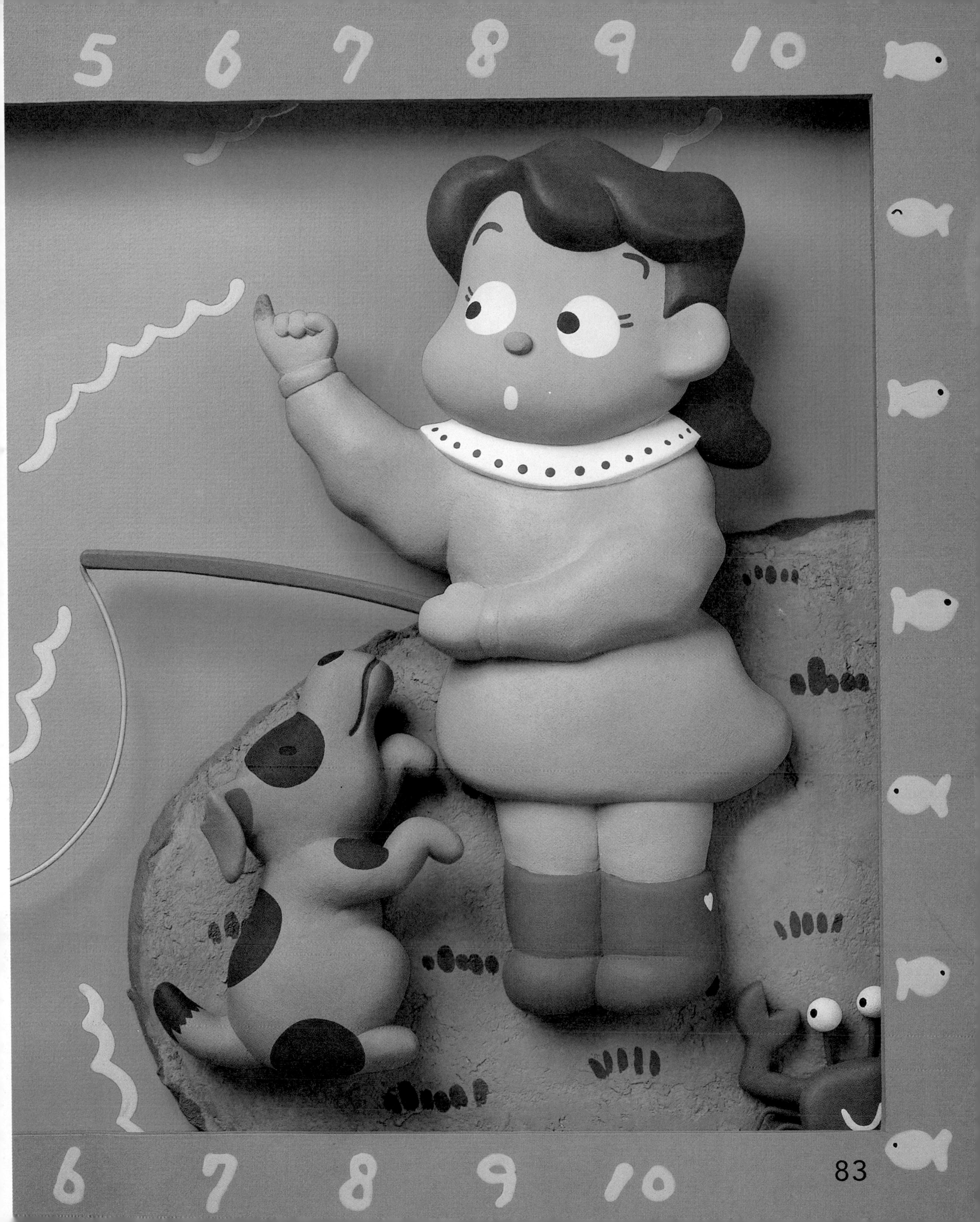
5 6 7 8 9 10
6 7 8 9 10

Family and Friends

Little pictures
Hang above me.
Pictures of the folks
Who love me.
Mom and Dad
And Uncle Jack,
They love me...
I love them back.

by Arnold Lobel

Words to Know

children	picture
come	your
family	dog
father	on
love	lots
mother	plan
people	click

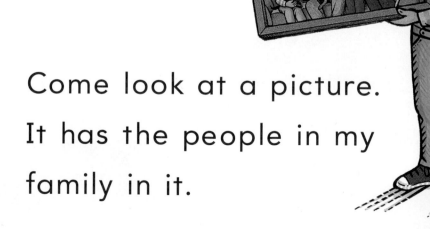

Come look at a picture. It has the people in my family in it.

It has my mother and father in it.

It has children in it.

It has six pets in it.

It has my black dog Pal on my lap.

We get lots of love.

Plan to get a big picture of your family.

Who will get in it?

Click, click, click!

Meet the Author
Sheila Kelly

Meet the Author and Photographer
Shelley Rotner

Who's in a Family?

written by
Sheila Kelly
and Shelley Rotner

photographs by
Shelley Rotner

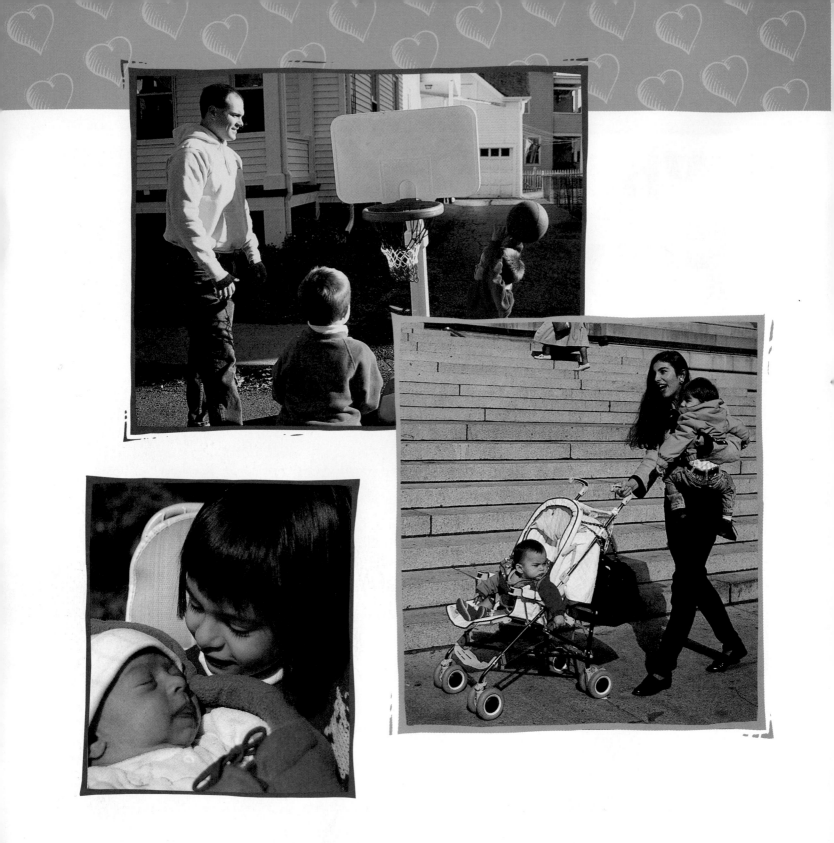

Who is in a family?
Quick! Come on! Let's see.

Let's snap a picture.
Click, click, click!

Sometimes a family is big.
Sometimes it is not.

Click, click, click!
A family can have a mother,
a father, and children.

Moms can hug.

Dads can hug, too.

People in families can get lots of love.

Click, click, click!
Families can have pets.

Here is a pet cat.

Here is a pet dog.

Click, click, click!

Here is a family in a big garden.

They can dig and pick lots of flowers.

Click, click, click!
Here is a family that jogs!
They can jog six quick laps
on a flat track.

Click, click, click!

Here is a family at a big picnic.

They can get hot food at the grill.

Click, click, click!

Here is a family tossing a big ball.

Quick, grab it! Toss it back!

Do not let it drop!

Here is a plan. Get set!
Quick! Get your family
in the picture.

Click, click, click!

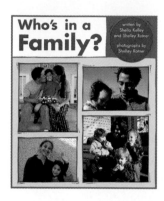

Who's in a
Family?

written by
Sheila Kelley
and Shelley Rotner

photographs by
Shelley Rotner

Think About the Story

1 How are the families the same?

2 How are they different?

3 Does your family do any of the things in the story? What are they?

104

Write a List

Write a list of some things that families like to do together.

Things Families Like to Do Together

fish

paint

cook

Good Night

Goodnight Mommy
Goodnight Dad

I kiss them as I go

Goodnight Teddy
Goodnight Spot

The moonbeams call me so

I climb the stairs
Go down the hall
And walk into my room

My day of play is ending
But my night of sleep's
 in bloom

by Nikki Giovanni

The Best Pet

The Best Pet
written and illustrated
by Anna Rich

Words to Know

friend	best
girl	Peg
know	pet
play	swell
read	ten
she	bells
sing	knock
today	Slim
write	wrist

My best friend is a girl called Peg. She has a pet called Slim Jim.

Read what I write to Peg today.

Does Slim Jim know
a swell trick?

Peg writes back.

Slim Jim can play a swell
trick. He can sit on my
wrist. Slim Jim can sing
and knock on ten bells.

Meet the Author and Illustrator
Anna Rich

The Best Pet

written and illustrated
by Anna Rich

My best friend is Peg.
Peg's pet is Slim.

Slim can sing.

Slim can play on big blocks.

One day I looked at a sign.
"Read it," I said to Peg.

"Write, Peg! Get Slim in the
Best Pet Test," I said.

"But what can Slim do well?"
she asked.

"I know. Here is a swell plan,"
I said.

Today is the Best Pet Test!

One girl had pet frogs who did a
trick in a box.

One boy had a pet dog who did a
trick on ten bells.

But Slim did the best pet trick.

Slim sat on Peg's wrist. Peg said,
"Knock! Knock!"

Slim asked, "Who's there?"

"Ben," said Peg.
"Ben who?" asked Slim.

"Ben knocking on your door
all day," said Peg.

Everyone smiled at Slim.
"It's the best pet trick!"

Slim got first prize!

The **Best Pet**
written and illustrated
by Anna Rich

Think About the Story

1 Why do you think the girls entered Slim in the Best Pet Test?

2 Do you think Slim did the best trick? Why?

3 What trick would you teach Slim for the Best Pet Test?

Write a Description

Write a sentence about your favorite character or pet from the story.

Slim is the best.

Knock-knock.
Who's there?
Cows go.
Cows go who?
Cows don't go who,
    they go moo.

Knock-knock.
Who's there?
You.
You who?
Are you calling me?

131

Words to Know

car	their	hug
down	walk	Bud
hear	would	fuss
hold	run	must
hurt	fun	scrub
learn	but	splat

Mom and Dad get in their big car. I can not hold Bud. "Walk," I tell Bud. "Do not run."

But Bud can not hear me.

Bud runs down to the car.

Splat! Bud is not hurt.

But I must scrub up.

I fuss. It is not fun.

"Bud, would you learn if you got a big hug?" I ask.

Meet the Author
G. Brian Karas

Meet the Illustrator
Clive Scruton

Bud's Day Out

written by G. Brian Karas

illustrated by Clive Scruton

Every day Ben would run in
and hug his dog, Bud.

Bud would run up and down,
but not today.

"Where is Bud, Mom? Is Bud
in back?" asked Ben.

"Let's look for him," said Mom.

"Is Bud hurt?" said Ben.

"Bud is not hurt," said Mom.

Ben got in their car.
"Hold on," said Mom. "Let's walk."

Ben and Mom walked.

"Did a big black dog run in?" asked Ben.

"Not today," said Dan.

"Why not stop in the glass shop?"

Ben and Mom walked.
"Did a big black dog run in?" asked Ben.

"Not today," said Jill.

"Why not stop in the pet shop?"

"Did you hear a noise, Mom?"
Ben asked. "I know where Bud is!"

What a big fuss!
Bud ran up and down.
The animals ran up and down.
Splat! Splat! Splat!

146

What a big mess!
"Stop! Stop! Stop!" yelled Mr. Plum.

"Come get a big hug, Bud," yelled Ben.
Ben got Bud. Bud got a big hug.

"Let's scrub up the mess," said Mom.
Mr. Plum felt glad.

"Bud must learn *The Ten Rules for Dogs*," said Mr. Plum.
Ben said, "Gee, what fun!
I can read. You can look at the pictures, Bud!"

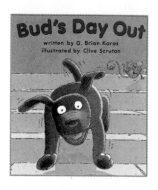

Think About the Story

1 How did Ben know where to find Bud?

2 Why did Bud need to learn rules?

3 What would you say to Bud?

Write a Sentence

Write a rule for Bud.

Do not run in the shop.

Where, Oh Where Has My Little Dog Gone?

Oh where, oh where has
   my little dog gone?
Oh where, oh where can he be?
With his ears cut short
   and his tail cut long,
Oh where, oh where is he?

Acknowledgments

For each of the selections listed below, grateful acknowledgment is made for permission to excerpt and/or reprint original or copyrighted material, as follows:

Poetry

"Good Night" from *Vacation Time, Poems for Children,* by Nikki Giovanni. Copyright © 1980 by Nikki Giovanni. Reprinted by permission of HarperCollins Publishers.

"Here We Are, Winter" from *Cricket Never Does,* by Myra Cohn Livingston, illustrated by Kees de Kiefte. Text copyright © 1997 by Myra Cohn Livingston. Reprinted by permission of Margaret K. McElderry Books, an imprint of Simon & Schuster Children's Publishing Division.

Selection from *Kids Are Punny 2: More Jokes Sent by Kids to "The Rosie O'Donnell Show".* Copyright © 1998 by The For All Kids Foundation. Reprinted by permission of The For All Kids Foundation.

"Little Pictures" from *Whiskers & Rhymes,* by Arnold Lobel. Copyright © 1985 by Arnold Lobel. Reprinted by permission of HarperCollins Publishers.

"Shiny Colored Tents" from *Cricket Never Does,* by Myra Cohn Livingston, illustrated by Kees de Kiefte. Text copyright © 1997 by Myra Cohn Livingston. Reprinted by permission of Margaret K. McElderry Books, an imprint of Simon & Schuster Children's Publishing Division.

"Sleeping Outdoors" from *Rhymes About Us,* by Marchette Chute, published in 1974 by E.P. Dutton. Copyright © by Marchette Chute. Reprinted by permission of Elizabeth Hauser.

Credits

Photography

3 (t) Ross Hamilton/Tony Stone Images. **7** (t) image Copyright © 2000 PhotoDisc, Inc. **12** (icon) Ross Hamilton/Tony Stone Images. **16** Andrew Yates/Mercury Pictures. **17** Richard Price/FPG International. **18** Donna Day/Tony Stone Images. **19** Mitch York/Tony Stone Images. **20** (t) Tim Davis/Tony Stone Images. (b) Daniel Cox/Tony Stone Images. **21** R.G.K. Photography/Tony Stone Images. **22** John Warden/Tony Stone Images. **23** Rob Casey/Tony Stone Images. **24** Lori Adamski Peek/Tony Stone Images. **25** Rommel/MASTERFILE. **26** Rommel/MASTERFILE. **27** (l) Jack Wilburn/Animals Animals. (r) Ted Levine/Animals Animals/Earth Scenes. **28** Chad Ehlers/Tony Stone Images. **29** Michael Agliolo/International Stock. **30** Gene Peach Photography/Liaison Agency. **32** Corbis Royalty Free. **33** Mug Shots/The Stock Market. **40** Courtesy Francisco Mora. **62** Norbert Wu Productions. **66-80** Norbert Wu Productions. **70** (shell) image Copyright © 2000 PhotoDisc, Inc. **84** (icon) image Copyright © 2000 PhotoDisc, Inc. **88** (t) © Shelly Rotner. (b) © Emily Calcagnino. **89–104** © Shelly Rotner. **110** Mike Tamborrino/Mercury Pictures. **128** image Copyright © 2000 PhotoDisc, Inc. **134** (t) Jon Crispin/Mercury Pictures. (b) Steve Benbow/Mercury Pictures. **152** image Copyright © 2000 PhotoDisc, Inc..

Assignment Photography

13, 34–5, 56–7, 81, 84–5, 105, 129, 153 David Bradley Photographer. **31, 63–5, 78–9** Michael Justice/Mercury Pictures.

Illustration

13–14 Chris Butler. **14–15, 16, 17–33**(bkgs) **34–35** Linda Helton. **36–37** Bonnie MacKain. **38–55** Francisco X. Mora. **58–59** Steve Henry. **60–79** Franklin Hammond. **82–83** Tomohiro Kikuchi. **86–87** Ruth Flanigan. **106–107** Siri Weber Feeney. **108–109, 111–127** Anna Rich. **130–131** Tim Haggerty. **132–151** Clive Scruton. **154–155** Martha Aviles.